FRANKENTHALER

New Paintings

FRANKENTHALER

New Paintings

May 1 – July 18, 2003

Knoedler & Company

— Established 1846 —

19 East 70 Street New York New York 10021

Tel 212 794-0550 Fax 212 772-6932

www.knoedlergallery.com

Bacchus
2002
acrylic on paper
60 x 74 3/8 inches

The Other Side
2002
acrylic on canvas
73 3/4 x 83 5/8 inches

Yoruba
2002
acrylic on paper
40$^1/_2$ x 60$^1/_2$ inches

Cloud Burst
2002
acrylic on canvas
79 1/2 x 68 1/4 inches

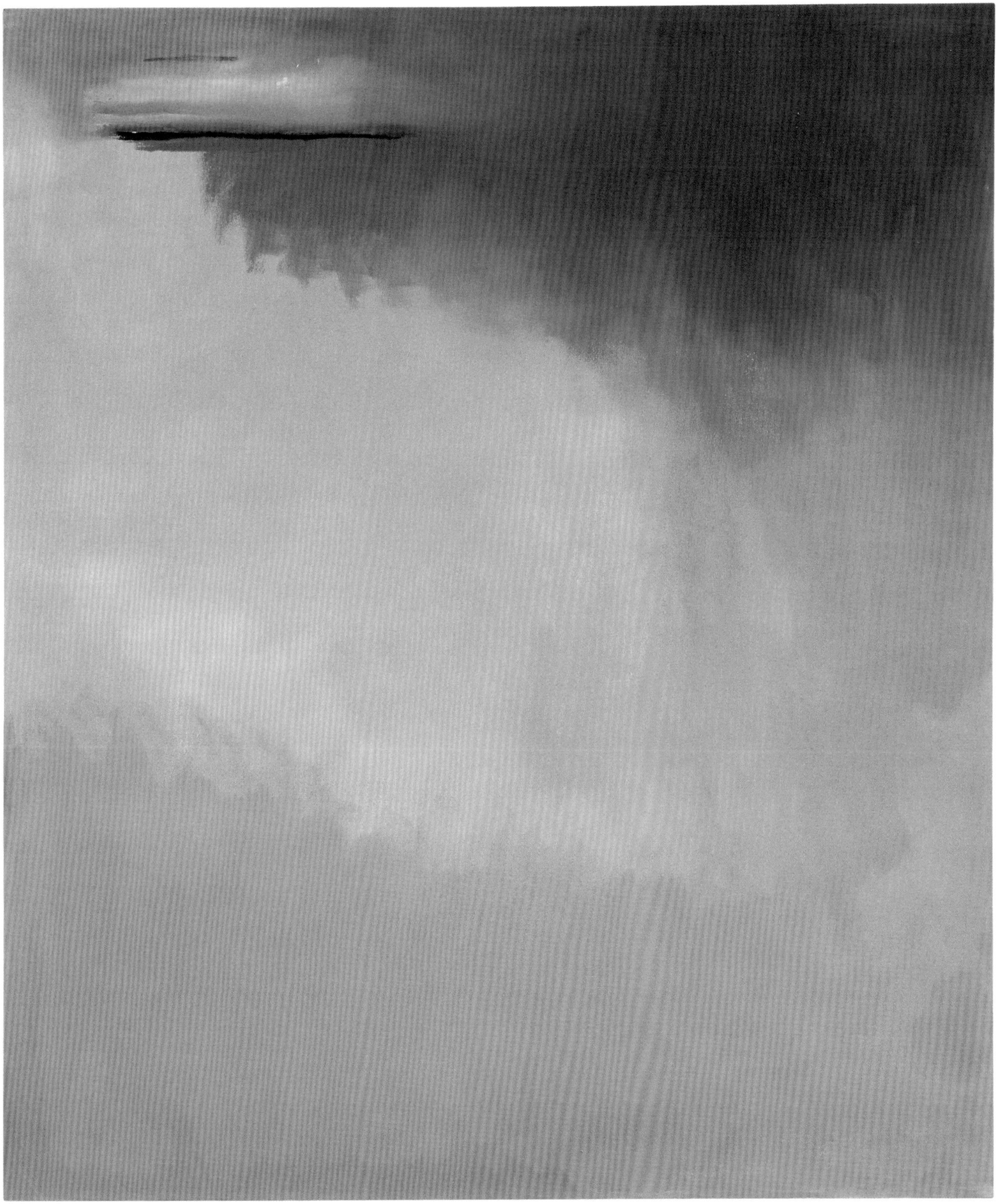

Almost Dark
2002
acrylic on paper
$40^{5}/_{8}$ x $60^{1}/_{2}$ inches

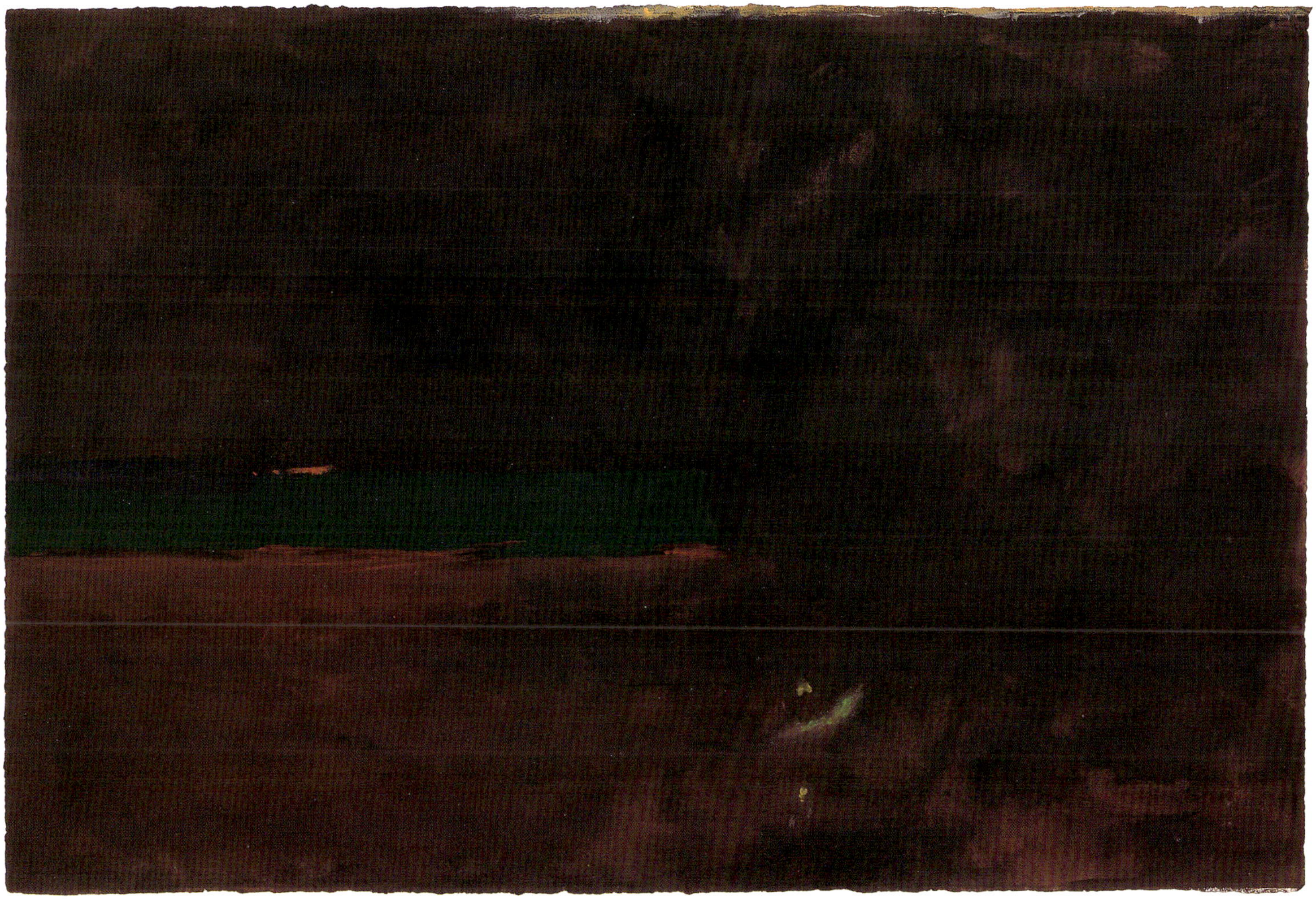

Southern Exposure
2002
acrylic on paper
60½ x 74 inches

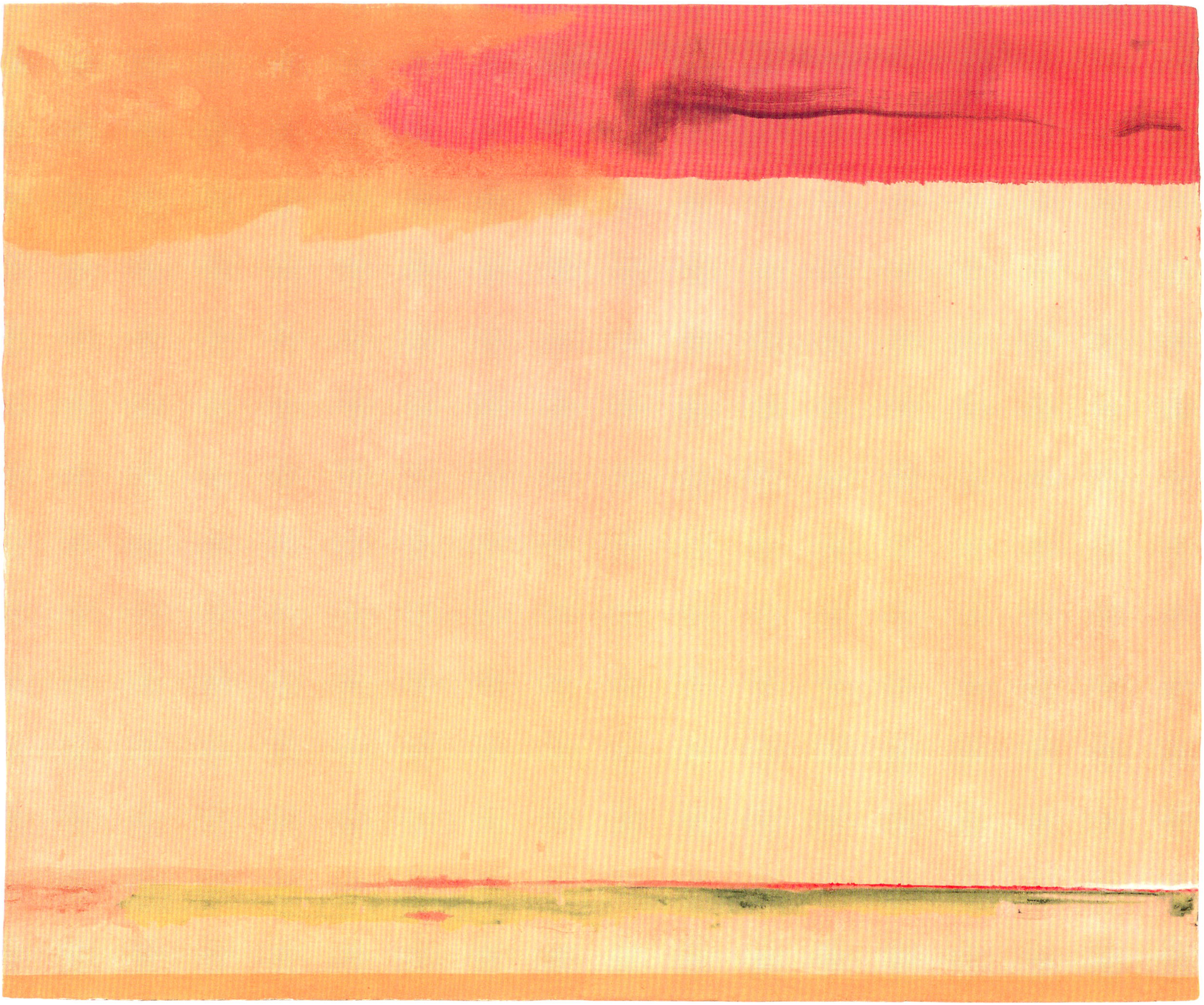

Vantage Point
2002
acrylic on paper
$40^1/_4$ x $60^3/_8$ inches

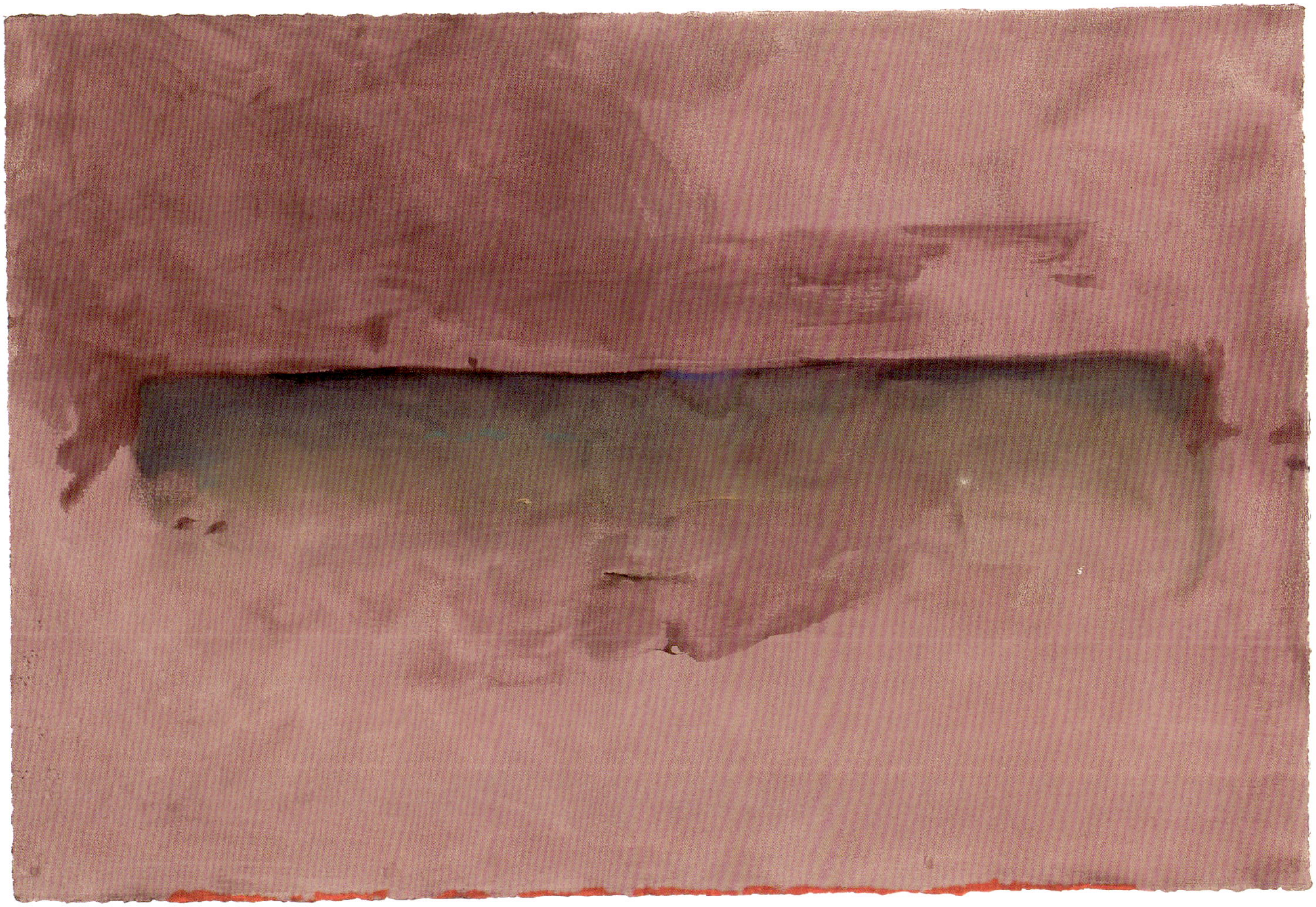

Driving East
2002
acrylic on canvas
52 1/8 x 81 1/2 inches

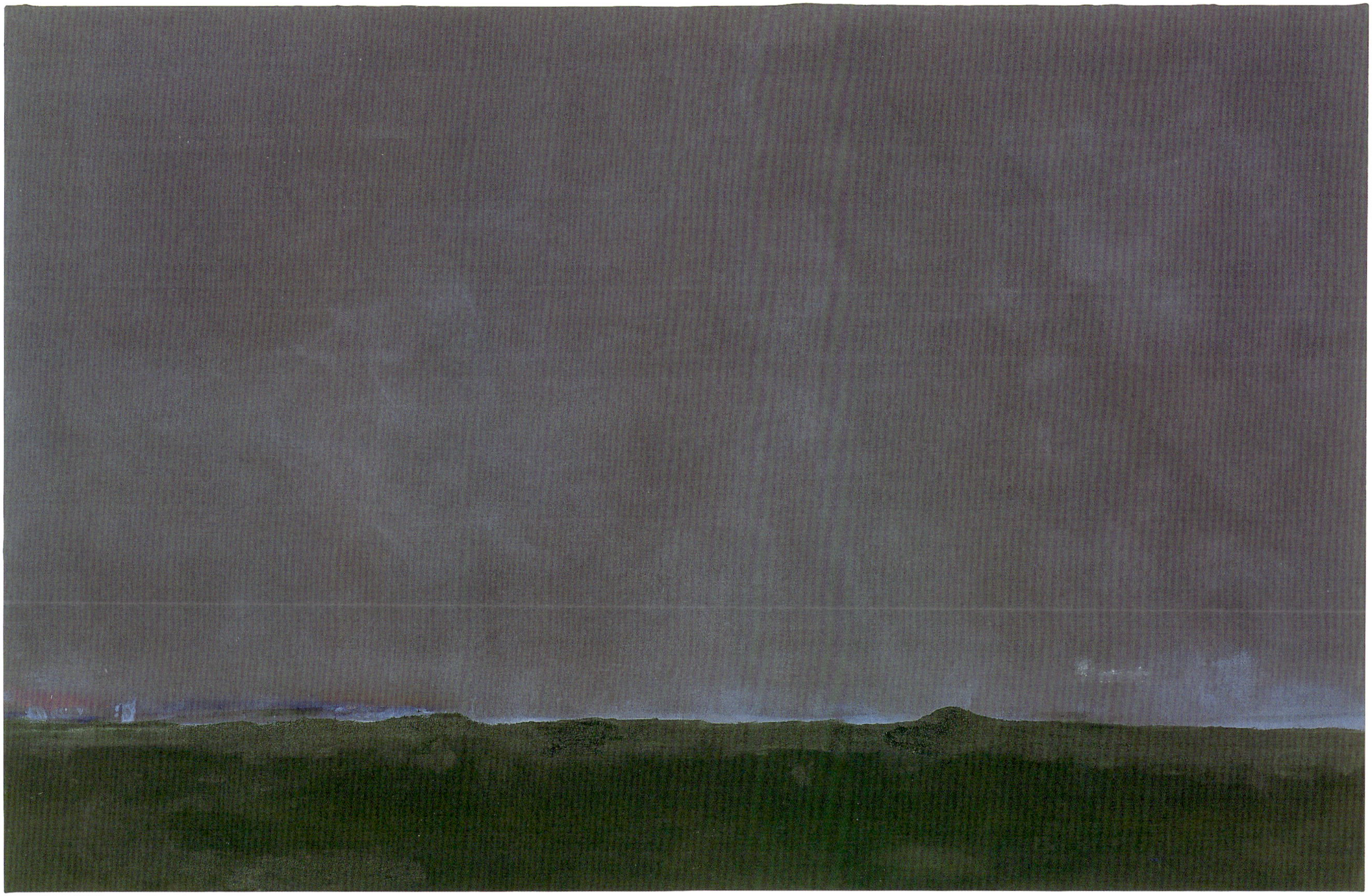

Ebbing
2002
acrylic on canvas
$52\frac{1}{8}$ x $81\frac{1}{2}$ inches

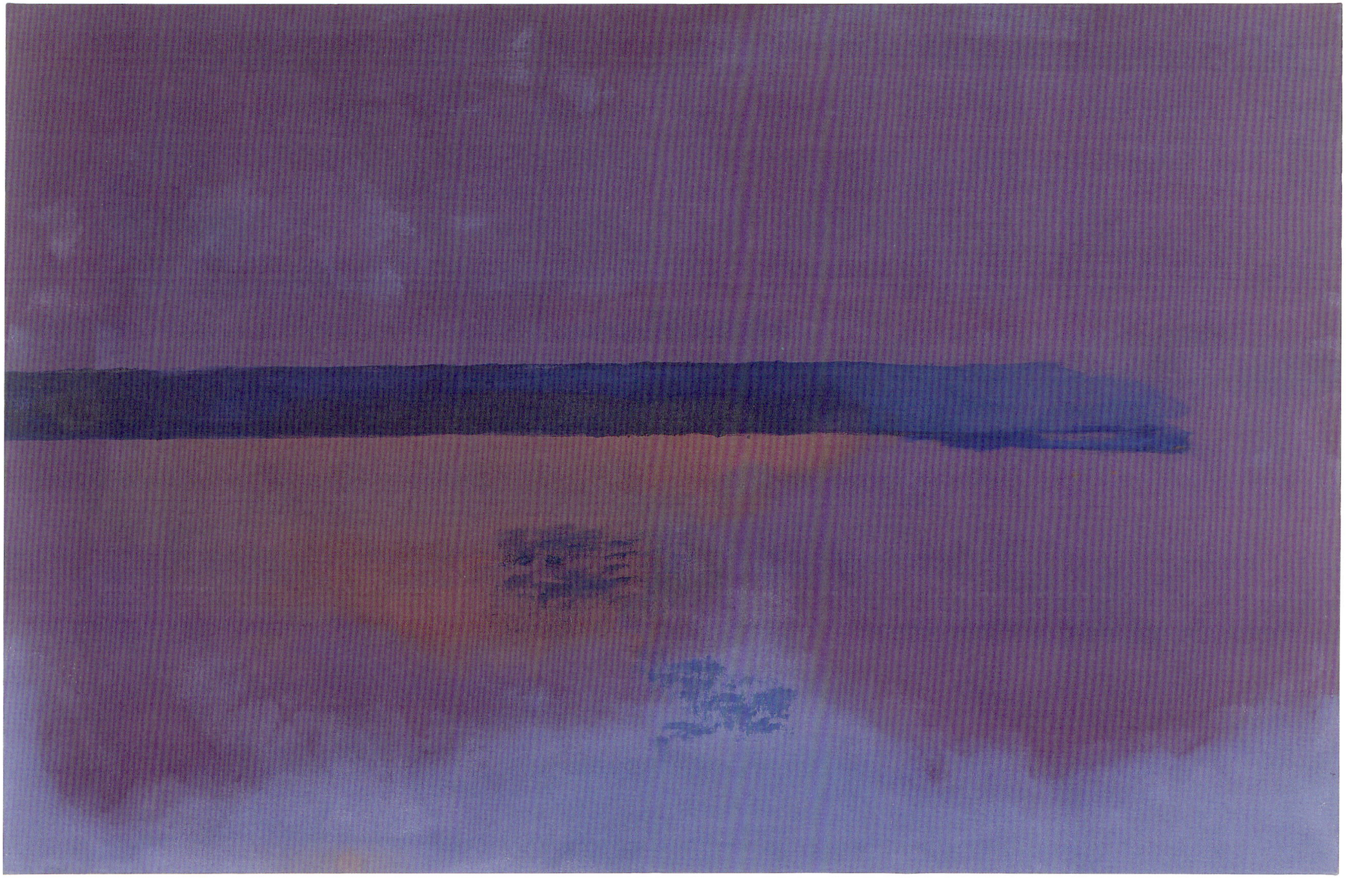

EXHIBITION LIST

Bacchus
2002
acrylic on paper
60 x 74 3/8 inches

The Other Side
2002
acrylic on canvas
73 3/4 x 83 5/8 inches

Yoruba
2002
acrylic on paper
40 1/2 x 60 1/2 inches

Warming Trend
2002
acrylic on canvas
74 3/4 x 84 1/4 inches

Cloud Burst
2002
acrylic on canvas
79 1/2 x 68 1/4 inches

Almost Dark
2002
acrylic on paper
40 5/8 x 60 1/2 inches

Southern Exposure
2002
acrylic on paper
60 1/2 x 74 inches

Vantage Point
2002
acrylic on paper
40 1/4 x 60 3/8 inches

Driving East
2002
acrylic on canvas
52 1/8 x 81 1/2 inches

Ebbing
2002
acrylic on canvas
52 1/8 x 81 1/2 inches

Published on the occasion of the exhibition

FRANKENTHALER

New Paintings

May 1 – July 18, 2003

Knoedler & Company

19 East 70 Street New York New York 10021

Tel 212 794-0550 Fax 212 772-6932

www.knoedlergallery.com

Color transparencies by Steven Sloman and Christopher Burke

Catalogue designed by The Grenfell Press, New York

Printed by Trifolio, Verona, Italy

ISBN: 0-9723207-4-1